SNOWBOARDING BLAST

SNOWBOARD BIG AIR

by Karen Grimaldos

CAPSTONE PRESS
a capstone imprint

Published by Capstone Press, an imprint of Capstone
1710 Roe Crest Drive, North Mankato, Minnesota 56003
capstonepub.com

Library of Congress Cataloging-in-Publication Data is available on the Library of Congress website.
ISBN: 9798875255724 (hardcover)
ISBN: 9798875255670 (paperback)
ISBN: 9798875255687 (ebook PDF)

Summary: Brave snowboard big air riders take high-flying tricks to the next level. Readers will learn about the sport's history, how tricks are scored, the most challenging tricks, and top stars of these competitions.

Editorial Credits
Editor: Carrie Sheely; Designer: Hilary Wacholz; Media Researcher: Rebekah Hubstenberger; Production Specialist: Tori Abraham

Image Credits
Associated Press: Anna Stonehouse/The Aspen Times, 21, Kyodo, 20, Pally Learmond/Red Bull Content Pool, 22; Getty Images: David Ramos, 4-5, 6, 8-9, 16, 23 (top left, middle right), Elsa, 29, Ezra Shaw, 26, Hannah Peters, 10, iStock/Artranq, cover, Lars Baron, 14, Lintao Zhang, 15, 18-19, Maddie Meyer, 23 (bottom left), Matthias Hangst, 24-25; Newscom: Matthias Trinkl/ZUMAPRESS, 27, Mitchell Gunn/Actionplus, 11, Rustin Gudim/ZUMAPRESS, 12-13; Shutterstock: PASTA DESIGN, 17

Design Elements
Shutterstock: AlexanderTrou, kostins, SAI A.D.A, Rosovskyi, sergio34

Printed and bound in China. 006459

TABLE OF CONTENTS

Words in **bold** are in the glossary.

CHAPTER 1

UP IN THE AIR

A snowboarder speeds down a steep **slope**. She goes faster and faster. She zips up a tall, long ramp. In seconds, she flies high into the air. She spins and flips.

Next, another brave rider does her run. During her amazing trick, she does a grab. Who will get the top score?

LET'S TALK SNOWBOARD BIG AIR!

backside: when a rider starts a rotation with their back turned, and they spin to face forward in the first quarter turn

cab: a trick where a rider starts by riding backward, spins, and lands standing the same way they started

cork: the combination of a rotation the rider does at an angle and a flip; the trick looks like a corkscrew

flip: a somersault in the air

frontside: when a rider starts a rotation with the front side of their body facing forward

grab: to hold on to the edge of a snowboard during a trick

rotation: a spin of the body in the air

run: a ride down the big air course

CHAPTER 2

BIG AIR BASICS

In 1994, a huge crowd gathered on a snowy mountaintop in Innsbruck, Austria. A tall ramp was set up nearby. Snowboarders sped down it. They performed amazing tricks after **launching** into the air. The crowd cheered! It was the first snowboard big air competition.

A rider competes at the World Championships in 2025.

FACT

Snowboard big air had become a world championship event by 2003.

Big air is all about big jumps! Why? The bigger the jump, the more time the rider has to do tricks. Snowboarders start their runs at the top of a huge ramp. Some are so tall, riders take an elevator to the top!

FACT

Big air riders can go as fast as 50 miles (80 kilometers) per hour in the air.

After sliding down the ramp, up they go! Some riders fly as high as 65 feet (15 meters) above the slope.

Now it's trick time! What tricks do riders do? Maybe a triple cork or a cab 1440. Any trick that **impresses** the judges will do!

Judges score tricks from one to 100 points. They want to see difficult tricks. They watch carefully to see how well riders perform the tricks. Judges also score based on **style**, jump height, and landings.

Yuka Fujimori competing in the 2018 Olympics

Top competitions are the Winter Olympics, the X Games, and the World Cup. In the World Cup, riders compete in several events during a **season**. At the season's end, the rider with the most points is the overall winner.

The top riders in a competition move on to the **finals**. They all have one goal—to win the gold medal!

Reira Iwabuchi competing at a World Cup event

FACT

Snowboard big air became an Olympic event in 2018.

SNOWBOARD BIG AIR GEAR

RAMP FEATURES

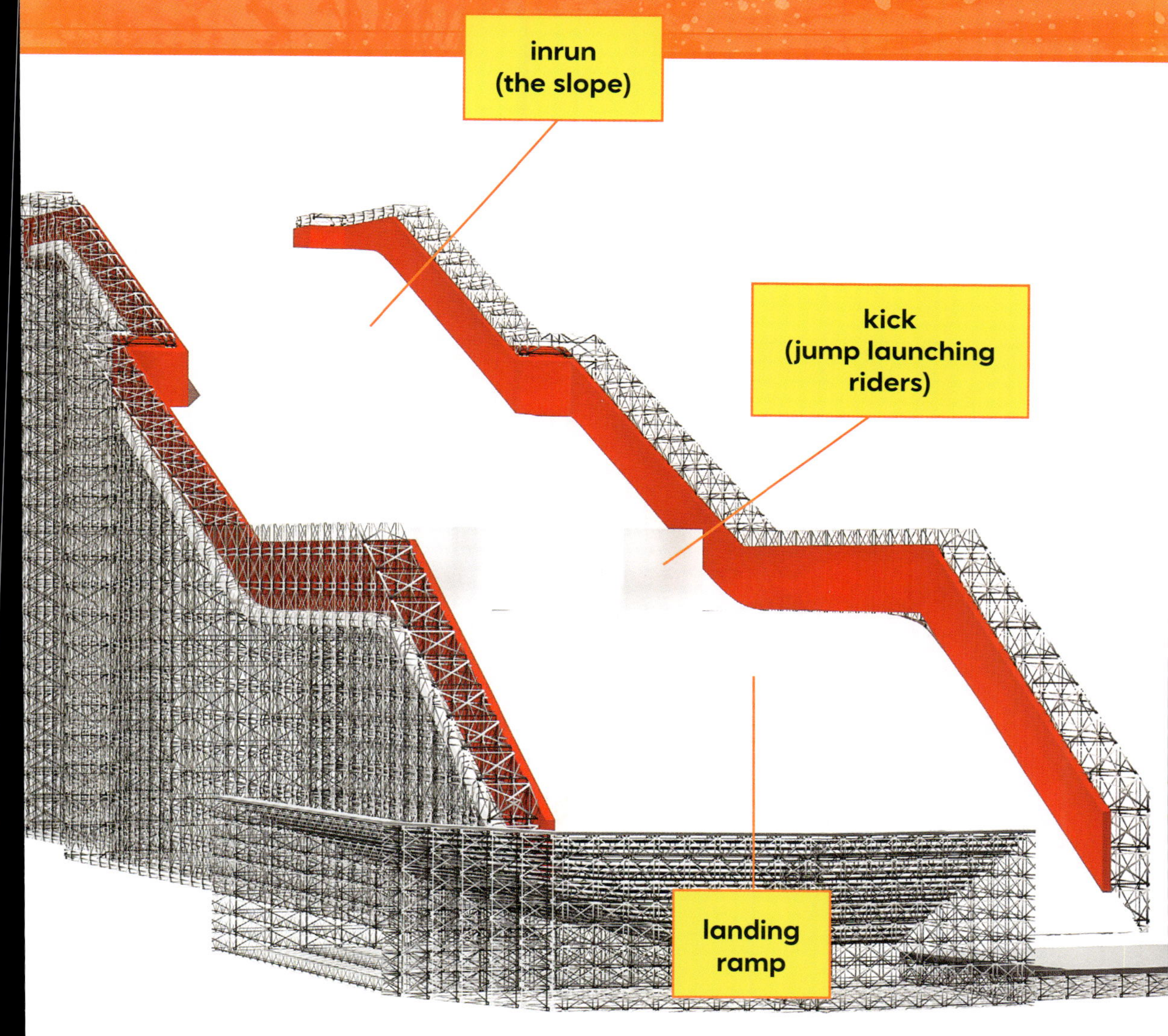

CHAPTER 3

WINNING MOVES

Competition is strong in big air. Scores can be close. Check out tricks top riders might do when every point matters!

One awesome trick is the frontside 1080. It has three full spins!

In 2017, Hailey Langland pulled off the first cab double cork 1080 in a women's competition. The crowd roared! For this trick, a rider completes two flips with three full spins. Wow!

In 2017, the cab double cork 1080 helped Hailey Langland (center) earn an X Games gold medal.

Few riders can do a cab triple 1260. In it, riders start riding backward. Then they complete three-and-a-half spins and land facing forward.

BOARD GRABS

Snowboarders use grabs to make their tricks more difficult. Difficult tricks often get more points from judges.

TAIL GRAB

The back hand grabs the tail of the board.

STALEFISH

The back hand grabs the heel edge of the board.

MELON GRAB

The front hand reaches behind the front leg and grabs the heel edge of the board. The hand is placed between both feet.

CHAPTER 4

BIG AIR'S BEST

Some pro riders lead the way in snowboard big air. Austrian rider Anna Gasser won gold medals in big air at the 2018 and 2022 Olympics. She won 10 big air World Cup competitions.

Anna Gasser competing at the 2018 Olympics

Hiroto Ogiwara competes at the 2025 X Games.

Japanese rider Hiroto Ogiwara made history at the 2025 X Games. He was the first rider to perform a 2340. He spun around six-and-a-half times!

British rider Mia Brookes has been riding since she was 18 months old! She was the women's overall World Cup winner for the 2023–2024 season. She won again the next season!

Mia Brookes holds a World Cup award in 2025.

FACT
Brookes was the first woman to land a cab 1440 in competition.

Su Yiming is a champion rider from China. He won the gold medal in a World Cup big air event in 2021. He went on to win the Olympic gold medal in big air in 2022.

Stars keep pushing the sport's limits. What thrilling tricks will they pull off next?

Su Yiming with the Olympic gold medal in 2022

GLOSSARY

finals (FI-nuhls)—the last round of competition

impress (im-PRES)—to make people think highly of you

launch (LONCH)—to take off into the air with great force

season (SEE-zuhn)—a part of the year where certain events or activities take place

slope (SLOPE)—an upward or downward slant

style (STILE)—the way something is done

READ MORE

Conaghan, Bernard. *Snowboarding.* New York: Crabtree Publishing, 2023.

Gaertner, Meg. *Snowboarding*. Mendota Heights, MN: Apex, 2022.

Goldstein, Margaret J. *Meet Chloe Kim*. Minneapolis: Lerner Publications, 2023.

INTERNET SITES

Hiroto Ogiwara
redbull.com/us-en/athlete/hiroto-ogiwara

Kiddle: Snowboarding Facts for Kids
kids.kiddle.co/Snowboarding

X Games
xgames.com

INDEX

ABOUT THE AUTHOR

Karen Grimaldos is a writer and educator who specializes in writing for the educational market. She loves writing for kids on topics ranging from art and culture to travel and current events. Although she doesn't snowboard, she does frequently dream of living in a place with snow-covered mountains.